Table Of Contents

Chapter 1: Introduction to ESG for Directors

Understanding ESG Principles

In today's rapidly evolving business landscape, the integration of Environmental, Social, and Governance (ESG) practices has become increasingly important for organisations looking to create long-term value and maintain their social license to operate. Directors play a crucial role in ensuring that ESG principles are effectively implemented within their organisations.

ESG principles are a set of criteria that investors use to evaluate a company's performance in key areas such as sustainability, social responsibility, and ethical governance. By taking a holistic approach to decision-making, companies can better manage risks, enhance reputation, and drive long-term growth.

For Non-Executive Directors, understanding ESG principles is essential for fulfilling their oversight responsibilities and providing strategic guidance to the board. By incorporating ESG considerations into board discussions, directors can help identify emerging risks and opportunities that may impact the organisation's long-term sustainability.

Charity Trustees also have a critical role to play in promoting ESG practices within their organisations. By aligning their charitable mission with ESG principles, trustees can demonstrate a commitment to ethical governance, social responsibility, and environmental stewardship.

Directors across all industries must recognise the importance of board diversity and inclusion in corporate governance. By bringing together individuals with diverse backgrounds, skills, and perspectives, boards can make more informed decisions and drive innovation in ESG practices.

In this chapter, we will explore the key principles of ESG and how they can be effectively integrated into corporate governance practices. By understanding the importance of ESG principles and their impact on long-term value creation, directors can better position their organisations for success in an increasingly complex and interconnected world.

Importance of ESG in Corporate Governance

In today's fast-paced and interconnected world, the importance of ESG (Environmental, Social, and Governance) practices in corporate governance cannot be overstated. Non Executive Directors, Charity Trustee's, and Directors play a crucial role in ensuring that companies are not only profitable but also sustainable and responsible in their operations.

ESG factors have a direct impact on a company's long-term performance and reputation. By considering environmental risks, such as climate change and resource scarcity, social issues like human rights and labor practices, and governance concerns such as board diversity and transparency, companies can mitigate risks, enhance their brand reputation, and attract investors who are increasingly looking for sustainable and ethical investments.

Board diversity and inclusion in corporate governance are essential components of effective ESG practices. By ensuring that board members come from diverse backgrounds and bring different perspectives to the table, companies can make better decisions, improve innovation, and enhance their ability to address ESG challenges.

Furthermore, integrating ESG practices into corporate governance can lead to improved financial performance. Studies have shown that companies with strong ESG practices tend to outperform their peers in the long run, as they are better equipped to adapt to changing market dynamics, attract top talent, and build strong relationships with customers and other stakeholders.

In conclusion, ESG practices are no longer just a nice-to-have for companies; they are essential for long-term success and sustainability. Non Executive Directors, Charity Trustee's, and Directors have a responsibility to prioritize ESG considerations in their decision-making processes and ensure that their companies are not only profitable but also responsible corporate citizens. By doing so, they can create value for all stakeholders and contribute to a more sustainable and inclusive future.

Overview of Environmental, Social, and Governance Practices

The chapter "Overview of Environmental, Social, and Governance Practices" provides a comprehensive look at the key principles and best practices in ESG for directors. In today's rapidly changing business landscape, it is essential for Non-Executive Directors, Charity Trustees, and Directors to understand the importance of incorporating ESG considerations into their decision-making processes.

Environmental, Social, and Governance (ESG) practices are becoming increasingly vital for companies looking to create long-term value and build resilience in the face of global challenges such as climate change, social inequality, and regulatory scrutiny. By integrating ESG factors into corporate governance, organisations can not only mitigate risks but also seize opportunities for innovation and growth.

This subchapter delves into the three pillars of ESG - environmental, social, and governance - and explores how they intersect with corporate governance. It provides practical insights on how directors can enhance board diversity and inclusion, drive sustainability initiatives, and improve stakeholder engagement.

Key topics covered include the integration of ESG considerations into strategic planning, the role of the board in overseeing ESG performance, and the importance of transparency and accountability in reporting ESG metrics. The subchapter also highlights case studies and best practices from leading companies that have successfully implemented ESG initiatives.

Overall, this subchapter serves as a practical guide for directors looking to navigate the complex landscape of ESG and drive positive change within their organizations. By adopting a holistic approach to environmental, social, and governance practices, directors can create a more sustainable and responsible business that benefits both society and shareholders.

Chapter 2: Corporate Governance and ESG

Role of Directors in Implementing ESG Practices

The role of directors in implementing ESG practices is crucial in today's corporate landscape. Non Executive Directors, Charity Trustees, and Directors play a pivotal role in driving environmental, social, and governance (ESG) practices within their organizations. As stewards of the company, directors have a responsibility to ensure that the organization operates in a sustainable and ethical manner.

One of the key responsibilities of directors in implementing ESG practices is setting the tone at the top. Directors must lead by example and actively promote a culture of sustainability and ethical behavior within the organisation. By demonstrating a commitment to ESG principles, directors can inspire employees, customers, and other stakeholders to embrace these practices as well.

In addition, directors must ensure that ESG considerations are integrated into the organisation's strategic planning process. This includes identifying ESG risks and opportunities, setting ESG goals and targets, and monitoring progress towards achieving them. Directors should also consider how ESG factors may impact the long-term viability and success of the organization, and incorporate these considerations into decision-making processes.

Furthermore, directors have a responsibility to oversee the implementation of ESG initiatives and ensure that they are effectively integrated into the organisation's operations. This may involve establishing ESG policies and procedures, allocating resources for ESG initiatives, and regularly monitoring and reporting on ESG performance.

Overall, directors play a critical role in driving ESG practices within their organisations. By championing sustainability, ethical behavior, and good governance, directors can help create long-term value for their organisations and contribute to a more sustainable and responsible business environment.

Integrating ESG into Corporate Strategy

In today's rapidly changing business landscape, integrating Environmental, Social, and Governance (ESG) practices into corporate strategy is becoming increasingly important for organisations looking to create long-term value and maintain a competitive edge. Non Executive Directors, Charity Trustee's, and Directors play a crucial role in ensuring that ESG considerations are embedded into the core of the company's operations.

Integrating ESG into corporate strategy involves aligning the company's values and goals with sustainability principles, responsible business practices, and ethical decision-making. This requires the Board to actively engage in discussions around ESG issues, set clear goals and targets, and monitor progress towards achieving them.

One key aspect of integrating ESG into corporate strategy is the recognition that environmental and social issues can have a significant impact on the company's long-term success. By incorporating ESG considerations into decision-making processes, the Board can help mitigate risks, identify opportunities for innovation, and enhance the company's reputation among stakeholders.

Board diversity and inclusion play a critical role in ensuring that ESG considerations are effectively integrated into corporate strategy. Diverse perspectives and experiences can help the Board better understand the social and environmental challenges facing the company, leading to more informed decision-making and improved performance.

Overall, integrating ESG into corporate strategy requires a holistic approach that considers the interconnectedness of environmental, social, and governance factors. By prioritising sustainability, responsible business practices, and ethical leadership, Non Executive Directors, Charity Trustee's, and Directors can help drive positive change within their organisations and contribute to a more sustainable and inclusive future.

Reporting and Disclosure Requirements for ESG

Reporting and disclosure requirements for ESG have become increasingly important for Non-Executive Directors, Charity Trustees, and Directors in today's corporate governance landscape. As stakeholders place greater emphasis on environmental, social, and governance practices, it is essential for organisations to be transparent about their ESG efforts.

One key aspect of reporting and disclosure requirements for ESG is the need for accurate and reliable data. Companies must collect and analyse data related to their environmental impact, social initiatives, and governance practices to provide stakeholders with a comprehensive view of their ESG performance. This data should be regularly updated and reported in a clear and accessible manner to ensure transparency and accountability.

In addition, reporting on ESG should go beyond mere compliance with regulations. Companies should strive to provide meaningful insights into their ESG performance, including the impact of their initiatives on stakeholders and the broader community. By telling a compelling story about their ESG efforts, organizations can build trust and credibility with investors, customers, and other stakeholders.

Furthermore, reporting and disclosure requirements for ESG should be aligned with best practices in corporate governance. Non-Executive Directors, Charity Trustees, and Directors should ensure that their organisations follow industry standards and guidelines for ESG reporting, such as the Global Reporting

Initiative (GRI) or the Sustainability Accounting Standards Board (SASB) framework.

Overall, reporting and disclosure requirements for ESG play a crucial role in enhancing transparency, accountability, and trust in corporate governance. By embracing these requirements and providing meaningful insights into their ESG performance, organisations can demonstrate their commitment to sustainability and long-term value creation.

Chapter 3: Board Diversity and Inclusion in Corporate Governance

Benefits of Board Diversity

Board diversity refers to the inclusion of individuals from a wide range of backgrounds, experiences, and perspectives on a company's board of directors. This diversity is essential for promoting innovation, creativity, and effective decision-making within an organisation. In the realm of corporate governance, board diversity has numerous benefits that can positively impact the overall performance and reputation of a company.

One of the key benefits of board diversity is the ability to access a wider pool of talent and expertise. By bringing together individuals with different skills, knowledge, and perspectives, companies can benefit from a more well-rounded and comprehensive approach to problem-solving and strategic decision-making. This can lead to more innovative solutions, increased competitiveness, and improved financial performance.

Board diversity also helps to enhance the overall governance of an organisation. By including individuals with diverse backgrounds and experiences, companies can better reflect the needs and interests of their stakeholders, including employees, customers, and shareholders. This can help to build trust and credibility with these groups, as well as improve the company's reputation and brand image.

Furthermore, board diversity can help to reduce the risk of groupthink and promote more robust decision-making processes. By encouraging healthy debate and constructive disagreement, diverse boards can avoid the pitfalls of group consensus and consider a wider range of perspectives when making important decisions. This can ultimately lead to better outcomes for the company and its stakeholders.

Overall, board diversity is a critical component of effective corporate governance and ESG practices. By embracing diversity and inclusion on their boards, companies can unlock numerous benefits that can help them to thrive in an increasingly competitive and complex business environment.

Strategies for Increasing Board Diversity

Diversity in the boardroom has become a hot topic in corporate governance discussions in recent years. Many studies have shown that diverse boards lead to better decision-making, improved financial performance, and overall better corporate governance. However, achieving diversity in the boardroom can be challenging, especially in industries where there is a lack of representation of certain demographics.

To increase board diversity, it is essential for directors and trustees to adopt specific strategies. One of the most effective ways to enhance diversity is to set clear diversity goals and targets for the board. By establishing measurable objectives, boards can track their progress and hold themselves accountable for achieving diversity.

Another strategy for increasing board diversity is to implement a formal board recruitment process that focuses on attracting diverse candidates. This process may involve using external search firms that specialize in diversity recruitment, as well as actively seeking out candidates from underrepresented groups.

Additionally, boards can promote diversity by fostering a culture of inclusivity within the organisation. By creating an environment where diverse perspectives are valued and respected, boards can attract and retain diverse talent.

Furthermore, boards can implement policies and practices that support diversity and inclusion, such as mentorship programs for underrepresented groups, unconscious bias training for board members, and regular diversity audits to track progress towards diversity goals.

Overall, increasing board diversity requires a concerted effort from directors, trustees, and other stakeholders. By adopting these strategies and actively working towards a more diverse and inclusive board, organisations can benefit from improved decision-making, better performance, and enhanced corporate governance practices.

Inclusive Practices for Board Decision Making

As Non-Executive Directors, Charity Trustees, and Directors, it is crucial to understand the importance of inclusive practices in board decision-making. In today's corporate governance landscape, diversity and inclusion are key components of effective decision-making processes. By incorporating diverse perspectives and voices at the board level, organisations can make more informed and ethical decisions that better reflect the needs and values of all stakeholders.

Board diversity and inclusion in corporate governance are not just about meeting quotas or ticking boxes. It is about creating a culture where all board members feel valued, respected, and empowered to contribute their unique insights and experiences to the decision-making process. Research has shown that diverse boards are more innovative, perform better financially, and are better equipped to navigate complex challenges and opportunities.

Environmental, social, and governance (ESG) practices play a crucial role in shaping inclusive board decision-making. By considering the environmental and social impacts of business decisions, boards can ensure that their organisations are operating in a sustainable and responsible manner. This not only benefits the planet and society but also enhances the long-term value and reputation of the organization.

In order to promote inclusive practices for board decision-making, boards should actively seek out diverse candidates for board positions, foster a culture of open dialogue and respect, and provide training and resources on diversity, equity, and inclusion. By embracing inclusive practices, boards can create a more ethical, transparent, and effective decision-making process that benefits all stakeholders.

Chapter 4: Environmental Practices in Corporate Governance

Implementing Sustainable Business Practices

Implementing sustainable business practices is essential for all organisations, regardless of size or industry. In today's world, stakeholders are increasingly focused on environmental, social, and governance (ESG) practices, and companies that fail to address these issues risk losing out on opportunities for growth and success.

Non-executive directors, charity trustees, and directors play a crucial role in driving sustainable practices within their organizations. By incorporating ESG considerations into their decision-making processes, these leaders can help create long-term value for their companies while also benefiting society and the environment.

One key aspect of implementing sustainable business practices is ensuring that the board of directors is diverse and inclusive. Research has shown that diverse boards are more likely to consider a broader range of perspectives and make better decisions when it comes to ESG issues. By promoting diversity and inclusion within their organizations, directors can help drive positive change and create a more sustainable future for all.

In order to effectively implement sustainable business practices, directors must also consider the environmental, social, and governance aspects of their operations. This may include reducing carbon emissions, promoting human rights and labor standards, and ensuring ethical business practices throughout the supply chain. By taking a holistic approach to ESG practices, organisations can enhance their reputation, attract top talent, and build trust with stakeholders.

Overall, implementing sustainable business practices is not only the right thing to do, but it is also a strategic imperative for organizations looking to thrive in today's rapidly changing business landscape. By prioritizing ESG considerations and fostering diversity and inclusion within their boards, directors can help drive sustainable growth and create a positive impact on society and the environment.

Addressing Climate Change Risks

Climate change is one of the most pressing issues facing businesses today, with the potential to significantly impact operations, supply chains, and overall financial performance. Non Executive Directors, Charity Trustees, and Directors play a crucial role in addressing these risks and ensuring their organisations are prepared for the challenges ahead.

One key aspect of addressing climate change risks is understanding the potential impacts on your organisation. This includes assessing how changes in temperature, extreme weather events, and shifting regulatory landscapes could affect your business. By conducting a thorough risk assessment, Directors can identify areas of vulnerability and develop strategies to mitigate these risks.

Board diversity and inclusion in corporate governance are also essential when addressing climate change risks. Diverse perspectives can lead to more robust discussions and better decision-making when it comes to implementing ESG practices. By including individuals with different backgrounds and experiences, boards can ensure that all potential risks and opportunities related to climate change are considered.

Implementing environmental, social, and governance (ESG) practices in corporate governance is another crucial step in addressing climate change risks. By integrating sustainability into your organisation's overall strategy, you can better position your company to adapt to changing environmental conditions and stakeholder expectations. This includes setting clear goals, tracking performance metrics, and regularly reporting on progress to stakeholders.

In conclusion, addressing climate change risks requires a proactive and comprehensive approach from Non Executive Directors, Charity Trustees, and Directors. By understanding the potential impacts, promoting diversity and inclusion, and integrating ESG practices into corporate governance, organisations can better prepare for the challenges ahead and create a more sustainable future for all stakeholders.

Managing Environmental Impact of Operations

Managing the environmental impact of operations is a crucial aspect of corporate governance in today's world. As Non-Executive Directors, Charity Trustees, and Directors, it is essential to understand the importance of incorporating environmental considerations into decision-making processes. This subchapter will provide practical guidance on how to effectively manage the environmental impact of operations within an organization.

One of the key steps in managing environmental impact is to conduct a thorough assessment of the organisation's current practices and their potential impact on the environment. This includes evaluating energy consumption, waste generation, and carbon emissions. By identifying areas where improvements can be made, directors can develop strategies to reduce their environmental footprint.

Implementing sustainable practices is another important aspect of managing environmental impact. This can involve adopting renewable energy sources, reducing water usage, and implementing recycling programs. By incorporating sustainability into the organization's operations, directors can not only reduce their environmental impact but also improve their reputation and attract environmentally-conscious stakeholders.

Furthermore, it is essential for directors to stay informed about current environmental regulations and best practices. By staying up-to-date on environmental issues, directors can ensure that their organisation remains compliant with relevant laws and regulations. This can help mitigate risks associated with non-compliance and demonstrate a commitment to responsible environmental stewardship.

Overall, managing the environmental impact of operations is a critical component of effective corporate governance. By incorporating environmental considerations into decision-making processes and implementing sustainable practices, directors can help create a more environmentally-friendly organization that is better positioned to thrive in a rapidly changing world.

Chapter 5: Social Practices in Corporate Governance

Stakeholder Engagement and Social Responsibility

Stakeholder engagement and social responsibility are crucial aspects of corporate governance in today's business landscape. Non-Executive Directors, Charity Trustees, and Directors play a key role in ensuring that their organizations are not only profitable but also socially responsible and environmentally sustainable.

Engaging with stakeholders, including employees, customers, suppliers, and the community at large, is essential for building trust and maintaining a positive reputation. By listening to the concerns and feedback of these groups, directors can better understand the impact of their decisions on various stakeholders and make more informed choices that benefit all parties involved.

Furthermore, social responsibility goes hand in hand with stakeholder engagement. Directors have a duty to ensure that their organisations are not only compliant with laws and regulations but also actively contribute to the well-being of society. This can include initiatives such as corporate social responsibility programs, charitable donations, and sustainable business practices that minimize the company's environmental footprint.

Incorporating environmental, social, and governance (ESG) practices into corporate governance is becoming increasingly important for organisations looking to attract investors, customers, and top talent. By prioritising diversity and inclusion in the boardroom, companies can benefit from a wider range of perspectives and ideas, leading to better decision-making and long-term value creation.

Overall, directors must recognize the importance of stakeholder engagement and social responsibility in today's business world. By taking a proactive approach to these issues, organisations can build stronger relationships with their stakeholders, enhance their reputation, and contribute to a more sustainable and equitable society.

Diversity and Inclusion in Workforce

Diversity and inclusion in the workforce are crucial components of successful corporate governance and ESG practices. Non-Executive Directors, Charity Trustees, and Directors play a vital role in promoting and fostering a diverse and inclusive workplace environment.

Diversity in the workforce not only brings different perspectives, experiences, and ideas to the table but also reflects the diverse customer base and communities that companies serve. By having a diverse workforce, companies can better understand and meet the needs of their stakeholders, leading to improved decision-making and innovation.

Inclusion, on the other hand, ensures that all individuals feel valued, respected, and included in the workplace regardless of their backgrounds, identities, or abilities. Inclusive work environments promote collaboration, creativity, and employee engagement, resulting in higher productivity and retention rates.

Non-Executive Directors, Charity Trustees, and Directors should actively support and advocate for diversity and inclusion initiatives within their organisations. They can do this by setting diversity and inclusion goals, implementing policies and practices that promote diversity and inclusion, and holding senior leadership accountable for progress.

Board diversity and inclusion in corporate governance are also important considerations. Having a diverse board of directors can lead to better decision-making, risk management, and overall corporate performance. Non-Executive Directors, Charity Trustees, and Directors should prioritise recruiting and retaining diverse board members who bring different perspectives and expertise to the table.

In conclusion, promoting diversity and inclusion in the workforce is not only the right thing to do but also beneficial for corporate governance and ESG practices. Non-Executive Directors, Charity Trustees, and Directors have a critical role to play in driving these initiatives forward and creating a more inclusive and equitable workplace for all.

Community Engagement and Philanthropy

Community Engagement and Philanthropy are crucial components of a company's Environmental, Social, and Governance (ESG) practices. As Non-Executive Directors, Charity Trustees, and Directors, it is essential to understand the importance of engaging with the community and giving back through philanthropic initiatives.

Community engagement involves building relationships with stakeholders in the local community, including employees, customers, suppliers, and government agencies. By actively engaging with the community, companies can gain valuable insights into the needs and concerns of local residents, as well as build trust and goodwill among key stakeholders. This can help to enhance the company's reputation and strengthen its social license to operate.

Philanthropy, on the other hand, involves donating time, resources, and money to charitable causes that align with the company's values and goals. By supporting charitable organisations and initiatives, companies can make a positive impact on society and contribute to the well-being of communities in need. This can also help to attract and retain top talent, as employees are more likely to be engaged and committed to a company that demonstrates a commitment to social responsibility.

Non-Executive Directors, Charity Trustees, and Directors play a key role in overseeing and guiding the company's community engagement and philanthropic efforts. By advocating for ESG practices in corporate governance, promoting board diversity and inclusion, and supporting environmental and social initiatives, these individuals can help to drive positive change within the organization and create long-term value for shareholders and stakeholders alike.

In conclusion, Community Engagement and Philanthropy are integral components of a company's ESG practices. By prioritising these areas and actively engaging with the community and supporting charitable causes, companies can enhance their reputation, build trust with stakeholders, and make a meaningful impact on society. Non-Executive Directors, Charity Trustees, and Directors have a critical role to play in guiding and overseeing these efforts, and by championing ESG practices in corporate governance, they can help to create a more sustainable and responsible business environment for all.

Chapter 6: Governance Practices in Corporate Governance

Board Oversight of ESG Practices

As non-executive directors, charity trustees, and directors, it is crucial to understand the importance of environmental, social, and governance (ESG) practices in corporate governance. The board plays a critical role in overseeing and guiding ESG initiatives within an organization, ensuring that they align with the company's values and long-term goals.

Board oversight of ESG practices involves setting the strategic direction for ESG initiatives, monitoring progress, and holding management accountable for their implementation. Non-executive directors, in particular, bring an independent perspective to the boardroom and can challenge management on ESG issues to ensure that they are being properly addressed.

In today's rapidly changing business landscape, it is essential for boards to prioritise ESG practices as part of their overall governance framework. By doing so, organizations can enhance their reputation, drive innovation, and create long-term value for all stakeholders.

Board diversity and inclusion also play a crucial role in effective oversight of ESG practices. Diverse boards are better equipped to understand and respond to the complex social and environmental challenges facing companies today. By incorporating a wide range of perspectives and experiences, boards can make more informed decisions that benefit both the organisation and society as a whole.

In this chapter, we will explore best practices for board oversight of ESG practices, including the role of non-executive directors, the importance of board diversity, and strategies for integrating ESG considerations into corporate governance. By taking a proactive approach to ESG, boards can drive positive change and create a more sustainable future for their organisations.

Executive Compensation and ESG Performance

In today's corporate landscape, the link between executive compensation and ESG (Environmental, Social, and Governance) performance is becoming increasingly important. Companies are realizing that aligning executive pay with ESG goals can drive positive outcomes for both the organisation and society as a whole. Non Executive Directors, Charity Trustee's, and Directors play a critical role in ensuring that executive compensation packages are structured in a way that incentivises sustainable business practices and long-term value creation.

When it comes to executive compensation, there are a few key principles that directors should keep in mind. First and foremost, compensation should be tied to performance metrics that reflect the company's commitment to ESG factors. This could include targets related to reducing carbon emissions, improving diversity and inclusion within the workforce, or enhancing corporate governance practices.

Incentivising ESG performance through executive compensation can help create a culture of accountability and responsibility within the organisation. By rewarding executives for achieving ESG goals, companies can drive positive change and demonstrate their commitment to sustainability and social responsibility.

Non Executive Directors, Charity Trustee's, and Directors should also consider the potential risks associated with tying executive compensation to ESG performance. It is important to strike a balance between incentivising positive behaviors and avoiding unintended consequences, such as short-term decision-making or greenwashing.

Overall, aligning executive compensation with ESG performance is a powerful tool for driving sustainable business practices and creating long-term value for all stakeholders. By incorporating ESG considerations into executive pay packages, companies can demonstrate their commitment to responsible business practices and position themselves as leaders in corporate governance, board diversity and inclusion, and ESG best practices.

Ethical Leadership and Corporate Culture

In today's rapidly changing business landscape, the role of ethical leadership and corporate culture has become more important than ever before. Non-Executive Directors, Charity Trustees, and Directors play a crucial role in shaping the ethical framework within their organizations, ensuring that environmental, social, and governance (ESG) practices are embedded in the corporate governance structure.

Ethical leadership is about setting the right tone at the top, demonstrating integrity, transparency, and accountability in decision-making processes. It involves leading by example, promoting a culture of trust and respect, and fostering a sense of social responsibility within the organisation. Non-Executive Directors, Charity Trustees, and Directors must act as role models for ethical behavior, championing diversity and inclusion in corporate governance practices.

Corporate culture, on the other hand, refers to the shared values, beliefs, and norms that guide the behavior of employees within an organization. A strong corporate culture that values ESG practices can lead to better business outcomes, increased stakeholder trust, and enhanced reputation. Non-Executive Directors, Charity Trustees, and Directors must work together to create a positive corporate culture that prioritises sustainability, social responsibility, and good governance.

By incorporating ESG practices into the corporate governance framework, organisations can drive long-term value creation, mitigate risks, and build resilience in the face of environmental, social, and governance challenges.

Non-Executive Directors, Charity Trustees, and Directors have a critical role to play in promoting ethical leadership and fostering a culture of sustainability within their organizations. By embracing ESG practices, they can help drive positive change, create a more inclusive and diverse boardroom, and ensure the long-term success of their organizations.

Chapter 7: Implementing ESG Practices in Corporate Governance

Developing an ESG Strategy

Developing an ESG strategy is crucial for Non-Executive Directors, Charity Trustees, and Directors who are looking to enhance their corporate governance practices. Environmental, Social, and Governance (ESG) factors are becoming increasingly important in today's business landscape, as stakeholders demand more transparency and accountability from organizations.

When developing an ESG strategy, it is important to first assess the current state of the organisation in terms of its environmental impact, social responsibility, and governance practices. This assessment will help identify areas for improvement and set the foundation for creating a comprehensive ESG strategy.

One key aspect of developing an ESG strategy is setting clear goals and objectives that align with the organisation's values and mission. These goals should be specific, measurable, achievable, relevant, and time-bound (SMART) to ensure accountability and track progress over time.

Another important step in developing an ESG strategy is engaging with stakeholders, including employees, customers, investors, and the community. By seeking input and feedback from these groups, organizations can better understand their expectations and priorities when it comes to ESG practices.

In addition, incorporating diversity and inclusion into corporate governance is essential for creating a more sustainable and socially responsible organization. By promoting diversity on boards and in leadership positions, companies can benefit from a wider range of perspectives and experiences, leading to better decision-making and performance.

Overall, developing an ESG strategy requires a commitment to continuous improvement and a willingness to adapt to changing stakeholder expectations. By prioritizing environmental sustainability, social responsibility, and good governance practices, organisations can build trust, enhance their reputation, and create long-term value for all stakeholders.

Monitoring and Evaluating ESG Performance

Monitoring and evaluating ESG performance is crucial for Non-Executive Directors, Charity Trustees, and Directors in ensuring that their organisations are meeting their environmental, social, and governance responsibilities. This subchapter delves into the various aspects of monitoring and evaluating ESG performance, providing practical guidance for those looking to enhance their organisation's sustainability practices.

One of the key components of monitoring and evaluating ESG performance is setting clear and measurable goals. Non-Executive Directors, Charity Trustees, and Directors should work with management to establish specific targets related to environmental impact, social responsibility, and governance practices. These goals should be closely aligned with the organisation's overall strategic objectives and should be regularly reviewed and updated as needed.

In addition to setting goals, monitoring and evaluating ESG performance also involves collecting and analysing relevant data. Non-Executive Directors, Charity Trustees, and Directors should work with management to identify key performance indicators (KPIs) that can be used to track progress towards ESG goals. This data should be regularly reviewed to ensure that the organisation is on track to meet its sustainability objectives.

Finally, monitoring and evaluating ESG performance also involves engaging with stakeholders. Non-Executive Directors, Charity Trustees, and Directors should communicate regularly with shareholders, employees, customers, and other key stakeholders to gather feedback on the organisation's ESG practices. This feedback can be used to identify areas for improvement and to demonstrate the organisation's commitment to sustainability.

By monitoring and evaluating ESG performance, Non-Executive Directors, Charity Trustees, and Directors can ensure that their organizations are meeting their environmental, social, and governance responsibilities. This subchapter provides practical guidance on how to set goals, collect data, and engage with stakeholders to enhance ESG performance and drive positive change within the organisation.

Continuous Improvement and Adaptation to ESG Trends

In today's rapidly changing business landscape, it is essential for Non Executive Directors, Charity Trustee's, and Directors to prioritize continuous improvement and adaptation to Environmental, Social, and Governance (ESG) trends. ESG factors are increasingly becoming critical considerations for businesses, investors, and stakeholders alike. As such, staying ahead of the curve and effectively integrating ESG practices into corporate governance is crucial for long-term success.

One key aspect of continuous improvement in ESG practices is the regular review and evaluation of current policies and procedures. Directors should regularly assess their organisation's ESG performance, identify areas for improvement, and implement necessary changes to align with evolving ESG trends. This may involve conducting ESG audits, engaging with stakeholders, and leveraging industry best practices to enhance sustainability and social responsibility efforts.

Furthermore, Directors must remain vigilant and adaptable to emerging ESG trends and regulatory developments. As ESG considerations continue to evolve, it is imperative for Directors to stay informed about the latest trends and developments in the ESG landscape. This may involve attending industry conferences, participating in ESG training programs, and collaborating with ESG experts to gain insights into emerging best practices and regulatory requirements.

Additionally, embracing diversity and inclusion in corporate governance is essential for driving ESG performance and fostering innovation. Research has shown that diverse boards are more likely to consider ESG factors and make better decisions that benefit all stakeholders. By promoting diversity and inclusion in the boardroom, Directors can leverage a wide range of perspectives and experiences to enhance ESG practices and drive sustainable growth.

In conclusion, continuous improvement and adaptation to ESG trends are essential for Directors to navigate the complex and dynamic ESG landscape. By prioritising ESG practices, embracing diversity and inclusion in corporate governance, and staying informed about emerging ESG trends, Directors can effectively drive sustainability, social responsibility, and long-term value creation for their organisations and stakeholders.

Chapter 8: Conclusion and Recommendations

Key Takeaways for Directors

As a non-executive director, charity trustee, or director, it is crucial to understand the importance of incorporating environmental, social, and governance (ESG) practices into corporate governance. These practices are not only essential for the sustainability and long-term success of a company but also for meeting the expectations of stakeholders and investors. Here are some key takeaways for directors to consider:

1. Board Diversity and Inclusion: Board diversity is crucial for effective corporate governance. Having a diverse board allows for a wider range of perspectives and experiences, leading to better decision-making and risk management. Directors should actively work towards increasing diversity and inclusion on their boards to ensure a well-rounded approach to ESG practices.

2. Understanding ESG Practices: Directors should familiarise themselves with the key ESG practices that are relevant to their industry and company. This includes understanding environmental risks, social impact, and governance structures. By incorporating ESG considerations into their decision-making processes, directors can better manage risks and opportunities.

3. Stakeholder Engagement: Directors should actively engage with stakeholders, including employees, customers, investors, and the community, to understand their expectations and concerns regarding ESG practices. By listening to and responding to stakeholder feedback, directors can build trust and enhance the reputation of the company.

4. Reporting and Transparency: Directors should ensure that the company's ESG practices are transparent and well-documented. This includes reporting on ESG performance, setting targets and goals, and monitoring progress over

time. By providing clear and consistent reporting on ESG practices, directors can demonstrate their commitment to sustainability and accountability.

In conclusion, incorporating ESG practices into corporate governance is essential for the long-term success and sustainability of a company. By focusing on board diversity and inclusion, understanding ESG practices, engaging with stakeholders, and promoting transparency, directors can effectively navigate the complex landscape of ESG and drive positive change within their organisations.

Best Practices for ESG Implementation

As non-executive directors, charity trustees, and directors, it is crucial to understand the best practices for implementing ESG (Environmental, Social, and Governance) practices within your organisation. ESG factors are becoming increasingly important in corporate governance, as they can have a significant impact on a company's long-term sustainability and success.

One of the key best practices for ESG implementation is to ensure that ESG issues are integrated into the overall corporate strategy. This means that ESG considerations should be taken into account when making strategic decisions, setting goals, and evaluating performance. By aligning ESG practices with the broader corporate strategy, companies can create value for all stakeholders while minimizing risks.

Another best practice for ESG implementation is to establish clear ESG policies and goals. Companies should develop specific policies that outline their commitment to ESG principles and set measurable goals for improving their ESG performance. These policies should be communicated to all employees, investors, and other stakeholders to demonstrate the company's commitment to sustainability and responsible business practices.

In addition, companies should regularly monitor and report on their ESG performance. This includes tracking key ESG metrics, conducting regular assessments of ESG risks and opportunities, and reporting on ESG performance to stakeholders through transparent and accessible channels. By measuring and reporting on ESG performance, companies can demonstrate their commitment to sustainability and accountability.

Overall, implementing best practices for ESG in corporate governance can help companies enhance their reputation, attract investors, and drive long-term value creation. By integrating ESG considerations into the corporate strategy, establishing clear policies and goals, and monitoring and reporting on ESG performance, non-executive directors, charity trustees, and directors can help their organisations navigate the complex landscape of ESG issues and build a more sustainable and responsible business for the future.

Resources for Further Learning and Development

As a Non-Executive Director, Charity Trustee, or Director, it is crucial to continue learning and developing your skills and knowledge in the areas of Corporate Governance, Board diversity and inclusion, and Environmental, Social, and Governance (ESG) practices. To help you further your learning journey, here are some valuable resources that you can explore:

Further Learning and Development Areas For readers interested in deepening their understanding of ESG in corporate governance, several avenues for further exploration are recommended: Sustainability Leadership: Examine the role of corporate leaders in driving ESG initiatives, including the development of sustainability competencies within boards.
Stakeholder Engagement: Investigate strategies for meaningful engagement with stakeholders on ESG issues, including community involvement, investor communications, and employee participation.
Emerging ESG Trends: Stay informed about evolving ESG trends, such as climate risk disclosure, social justice considerations, and the integration of sustainable finance.
Technology and Innovation: Explore how technological innovations, including

AI and blockchain, are being leveraged for ESG data tracking, reporting, and improvement.

Recommended Resources
To facilitate further learning, the following resources are invaluable:
Websites: Sustainable Accounting Standards Board (SASB): sasb.org
Global Reporting Initiative (GRI): globalreporting.org
CDP (formerly Carbon Disclosure Project): cdp.net

Reading Material: "ESG for Boards: A Guide to Integrating ESG into Corporate Governance" by L. Heidrich & S. Ward. This book provides practical advice for boards on incorporating ESG into governance frameworks. "Principles for Responsible Investment (PRI)": Access a wealth of reports and guides on ESG investing practices at unpri.org.

CPD Modules: "Integrating ESG into Corporate Strategy" by the Harvard Business School Online offers a course that helps leaders understand and implement ESG principles.

"Sustainability and ESG: A Strategic Leadership Approach" available on Coursera, hosted by the University of Illinois, focuses on developing leadership skills for sustainability.

Professional Networks and Forums: ESG-focused LinkedIn groups such as "ESG Reporting and Communications" provide platforms for professionals to exchange knowledge, challenges, and solutions.
Annual ESG conferences and webinars hosted by financial and sustainability organisations offer opportunities to hear from experts and network with peers.

By utilising these resources for further learning and development, you can stay ahead of the curve and make informed decisions that contribute to the success and sustainability of your organisation. Remember, continuous learning is key to being an effective and responsible director or trustee in today's rapidly changing business landscape.

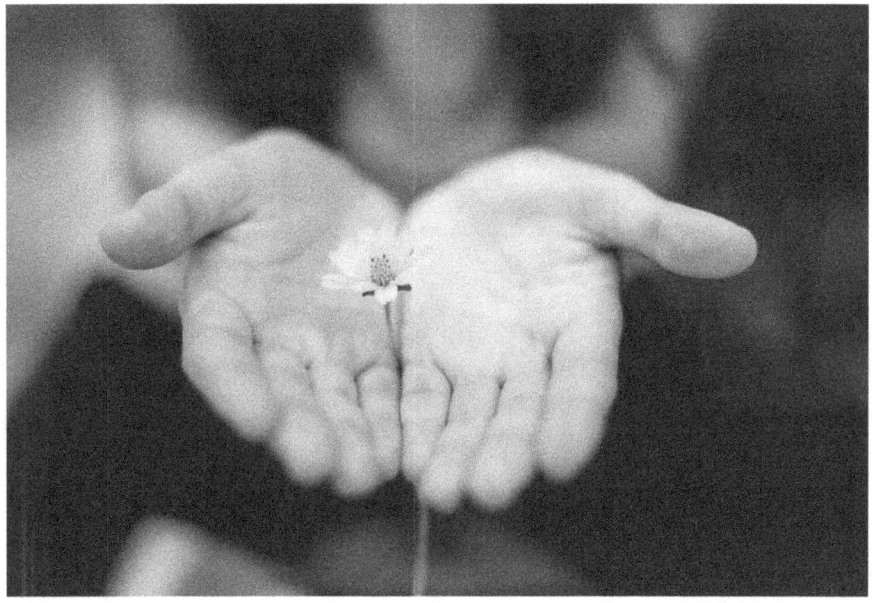

www.ingramcontent.com/pod-product-compliance
Lightning Source LLC
Chambersburg PA
CBHW070454290526
45791CB00005B/2129